GW00634843

opqrstuvwxyz

First published 1984 by
Walker Books Ltd
184-192 Drummond Street
London NW1 3HP

© 1984 John Burningham

First printed 1984
Printed and bound by
L.E.G.O., Vicenza, Italy

British Library Cataloguing in Publication Data
Burningham, John
Jangle twang.——(John Burningham's first words)
I. Title   II. Series
823'.914 [J]   PZ7

ISBN 0-7445-0169-5

jangle twang

John Burningham

WALKER BOOKS
LONDON

boom

clash

scrape

blare

tinkle

strum

pluck

rattle

squeak

jangle

toot

blast

wail

ping

sing

abcdefghijklmr